The Author

Derek Walters is one of the few practising specialists of
Chinese Astrology in the Western hemisphere.

Born in the Year of the Fire-Rat, during the Wood-season,
in a Dragon-month, he takes his opportunism from the
Rat, the Wood accounts for his creative side, and the Fire,
a scientific leaning; while the influence of the Dragon is
the stimulus for his interest in astrology.

Text Copyright © Derek Walters 1988

Compilation Copyright © Pagoda Books 1988

Illustrations: Endpapers, from a Chinese horoscope calendar for
the year 877, courtesy The British Library; p.17, from a Ming Encyclopedia,
dated 1610; page 29, the character for happiness; and page 33, the three
symbols for happiness, dignities and longevity from Researches into
Chinese Superstitions by H. Doré, Shanghai, 1917.

ISBN 0946326 64 9

Printed in Great Britain by
Purnell Book Production Limited

Cast Your Chinese Horoscope

THE

HORSE

D E R E K   W A L T E R S

Contents

Introduction

*O*ur Destiny! Are we the rulers of our Fate? Are our lives shaped merely by chance circumstances? Or is the future already mapped out for us?

Few people, whatever their beliefs, could honestly say that future events hold little interest for them. Millions of readers worldwide turn to the astrological columns in their newspapers ever day; while at fairs and festivals, fortune-tellers are always sure to be a popular attraction. For the Chinese, meanwhile, a consultation with the seer at the local temple is traditionally regarded a serious matter, not to be undertaken lightly. Indeed, on any day of the week – morning, afternoon and night – Chinese temples, such as the Wong Tai Sin in Kowloon or the ancient Lung Shan in Taipei, are filled with throngs of devout worshippers, who have come to enquire from the monks what the prospects are for future happiness, security, and health.

In ancient times, astrology was a highly secret art, for it was thought that the movements of the stars were messages from the gods to the Emperor, and thus far too important for the eyes and ears of common folk. Every person at the court was represented by one of the stars in the Heavens: and the Emperor's, of course, was the Pole Star, round which, as Confucius said, 'all the other stars make obeisance.' The stars closest to the Pole Star represented the Emperor's family, while round them rotated the stars of the ministers, generals, and nobility. As they twinkled, glimmered or faded, so the fortunes of the court officials were revealed.

With the growth of the Chinese empire, its traders and merchants grew more prosperous; and although they were not important enough to have their own stars in the sky, they were sufficiently well-off to persuade the temple monks to cast their horoscopes for them. It was a crime punishable by death for anyone other than the official court astrologers to study the heavens, but the monks were clever enough to realise that the motions of the stars and planets were sufficiently regular and ordered to enable them to calculate horoscopes based solely on the day of birth. Accordingly, a new branch of astrology developed in China — *Ming Shu*, meaning literally 'the reckoning of Fate'.

In the course of time, the temple astrologer began to play a role as important as a registrar of births, marriages and deaths, and these were the occasions when he was most likely to be in demand: and today, too, Chinese temples have their forecourts and side booths where the temple astrologers can be consulted. Even in mainland China, where 'superstitious practices' are frowned upon by the authorities, orange-robed priests sit patiently in the quiet temples, deftly applying brush-stroke calligraphy to the red paper horoscopes which are still eagerly sought after by the faithful few. In Taiwan, too, old traditions are carefully maintained as a way of life. There, at the great temples, so many astrologers are busy working that their booths overflow the temple grounds into the streets and the subway below, where many of them even have their own private telephones!

According to Chinese tradition, when a child is born, an astrologer is called on to cast horoscopes, and this is usually sealed and kept in a special box throughout the child's life. Often, too, marriages will not be contracted between two families until both parties have consulted their astrologers to ensure that the couple's horoscopes show that they are a compatible pair.

On New Year's Day, Chinese families from Hong Kong to San Francisco, whether or not they are able to go to the expense of employing a professional astrologer to see what the coming year holds in store for them, will certainly buy the new yearly almanac. This is hung at home in a prominent place, where it can be consulted for daily directions and advice on almost every conceivable action, from digging trenches to washing hair. (This might seem odd to the western reader at first; but in fact the western world also has many similar customs with traditional days for doing the laundry, going to market – and even for eating fish or turkey!) The Chinese pay great attention to the almanac's instructions, not just for social convenience, but because it is believed that the penalties for ignoring such daily directions include dire punishment in the world-to-come.

The twelve animals of Chinese astrology

The ancient Chinese first began to study astrology many thousands of years ago, centuries or more before they had made contact with the West: so that by the time that a thriving trade had opened up across the vast continent of Asia, their system of astrology was already firmly established, with quite a different form from the western practice. Even the patterns of stars which shape the constellations were seen quite differently by the ancient Chinese: and the names given to the constellations are significantly different, too. Whereas in the West, many of the names of the stars and constellations have a nautical touch about them, suggesting that the stars were given their names by a people who lived near the sea or who were sea-faring, many Chinese star names, on the other hand, refer to horses and carriages, suggesting a nation that was more at home inland than on the water.

But the most noticeable difference lies at the very heart of popular astrology. In the West, when someone asks about your star-sign, he is really asking which *month* you were born in. The Chinese, however, like to know what *year* you were born in. The twelve animals of Chinese astrology – the so-called 'Chinese Zodiac' – are used to name the different years in one Great Year of twelve ordinary years. So, according to your particular year of birth, you may be a Rat, Ox, Tiger or Hare; a Dragon, Snake, Horse or Sheep; a Monkey, Rooster, Dog or Pig.

How, when, or why these animals were chosen to represent their particular years is a mystery which perplexes scholars to this day. Legend says that the Buddha summoned all the animals, and that these twelve were the only ones which answered. It is more likely, however, that these animal names were carefully chosen by ancient astrologers because they seemed to be the best ones to represent the characteristics of people born in those years, and also indicated what the events of coming years might be like.

As you become acquainted with the characteristics of each animal year, remember that the Chinese interpretation is often very different from western ideas. Some people find it far from flattering to learn that they were born in Rat or Pig years, for example: but to the Chinese, the Rat is the symbol of ingenuity; and the Pig, a sign of comfort. You can discover more about your own animal type on pages 17-20; while if you turn to the section beginning on page 21, you will find how you are likely to fare in each different animal year.

Yin and Yang signs

The twelve animal signs are conveniently grouped into six pairs – the first of each pair considered to have *yang* or active attributes, the second possessing softer *yin* qualities. Thus, the creative Rat is paired with the practical Ox; the competitive Tiger with the diplomatic Hare; the exuberant Dragon with the prudent Snake; the convivial Horse with the rather astute Rooster; and the faithful Dog with the caring Pig.

According to Chinese beliefs, all things are made from differing proportions of *yin* and *yang*. It is even sometimes said that these two forces correspond to 'female' and 'male'; but in reality, they are only terms of convenience. Thus in any one personality, *yin* and *yang* represent the opposing sides of human character, the passive and the active, the imaginative and the logical, as well as the creative and the destructive.

Personality revealed

Each pair of animal signs further combines to form one of the six aspects of destiny known to astrologers as 'Houses.' Not only do these help to paint a character portrait, they also reveal the likely trends of fortune for different periods of time – years, months, days, or hours – which are associated with each animal.

The Rat and Ox represent beginnings and completions of projects in the *House of Construction*; the Tiger and the Hare symbolise the aggressive and diplomatic paths to personal achievement in the *House of Expansion*; the Dragon and the Snake reflect the extrovert and introspective sides of personality in the *House of Mystery*; the Horse and Sheep reveal the basic differences in interests shown by both sexes in the *House of Gender*; craftsmanship and flair are the two qualities essential to success represented by the Monkey and the Rooster in the *House of Career*; and finally, the Dog, symbolising friendship and protection, and the Pig symbolising the home, its comforts, and also offspring, belong to the *House of Family*.

Many people, when they first encounter Chinese astrology, find it hard to accept the general principle that everyone born in a particular year will have the same basic characteristics. But in fact this is one of Chinese astrology's most convincing factors: and teachers, in particular, are very apt to observe that each school year's intake seems to have its own inherent characteristics.

There are also a number of ways by which the general characteristics of each animal-type can be refined to give a detailed character assessment of each individual. For just as anyone familiar with western astrology will know that the hour of birth reveals the 'ascendant' of the horoscope, the Chinese consider that the time at which person was born has an important bearing on future career and happiness. Other aspects which help to paint a more accurate picture of personality and fate are given by the month or season of birth: and the animal-types associated with each month may either strengthen or weaken the characteristics of the year-type. Thus, someone born in a Rat year would have his Rat characteristics emphasized if born in a Rat month, but toned down if born in the Horse month – the Rat's opposite sign. The Chinese calendar is regulated by the phases of the Moon, and is therefore extremely complicated; but you will be able to get a good idea of which animal is associated with your particular birth month from the table on page 12.

Compatibility between animal types

Once you are familiar with your own animal sign, you will no doubt want to know the signs of others close to you, and then to establish the nature and extent of your compatibility.

There is a simple way to do this. If the names of the twelve animals are placed in order (Rat, Ox, Tiger, Hare, Dragon, Snake, Horse, Sheep, Monkey, Rooster, Dog, Pig) at the twelve positions of the hours of a clock-face, with your own birth-year animal at the twelve o'clock position, then the most compatible signs will be at the four o'clock and eight o'clock positions, compatible signs at two and ten o'clock, poor compatibility at three and nine o'clock, and adversity shown at the six o'clock position.

The Twelve Chinese Months and their Associated Animals

First month   approximating to February: *the Tiger*

Second month   approximating to March: *the Hare*
(The Hare month includes the Spring Equinox)

Third month   approximating to April: *the Dragon*

Fourth month   approximating to May: *the Snake*

Fifth month   approximating to June: *the Horse*
(The Horse month includes the Summer Solstice)

Sixth month   approximating to July: *the Sheep*

Seventh month   approximating to August: *the Monkey*

Eighth month   approximating to September: *the Rooster*
(The Rooster month includes the Autumn Equinox)

Ninth month   approximating to October: *the Dog*

Tenth month   approximating to November: *the Pig*

Eleventh month   approximating to December: *the Rat*
(The Rat month includes the Winter Solstice)

Twelfth month   approximating to January: *the Ox*

Broadly-speaking, the most compatible signs fall into four groups of three: the Rat, Dragon, and Monkey; the Ox, Snake, and Rooster; the Tiger, Dog and Horse; and the Pig, Hare and Sheep. More detailed remarks on your relationships with other people, whether in business, within the family, in friendship or in romance, can be found on pages 25-28.

But to make a more specific comparison of two personalities, it is also important to take into account the interaction of the Five Elements.

The Five Elements

The Chinese sages of old taught that the Universe is kept in order by Five Elements – Wood, Fire, Earth, Metal and Water – and that one gives rise to the next in regular succession, or as the Chinese say: 'Wood burns, producing Fire; Fire leaves ash – or Earth – from which Metal is mined; Metal melts, like Water; and Water feeds growing Wood'; after which the whole cycle begins again.

Similarly, the order of the Five Elements can be likened to the progress of the year as it passes through five 'seasons', each associated with one of the elements. Spring, season of growth and creation, belongs to Wood; the hot season is governed by

Fire; the middle of the year, by the Earth element; the harvest, when ploughs cut into the Earth, by Metal; and finally, the cold, wet season, by Water.

In the Chinese calendar, years are counted in pairs according to the elements. Thus 1984 and 1985 were ruled by the Wood element, 1986 and 1987 by the Fire element, and so on. In this way, each year has both an animal name and an element; so that someone born in a particular year can be described not only as a particular animal type but also by the relevant element. This makes it possible to outline character assessments in greater detail: and just how the five elements influence your own particular animal sign is explained more fully on pages 19-20.

Compatibility between the element types

The usual order of the Five Elements is the 'generative' order, in which each element 'generates' the next in the series: and as a general rule, it can be said that two people will be compatible if their influencing elements stand in the generative order – a Wood-type and a Water-type, for instance. But there is also a 'destructive' order (Wood – Earth – Water – Fire – Metal), in which each successive element overpowers the other, and such combinations are usually found to be less fortunate. (Wood is said to absorb the goodness from Earth; Earth sullies Water; Water quenches Fire; Fire melts Metal; and Metal chops down Wood.)

From these two orders, it is easy to imagine how one element type may either help or hinder another. Positively, a Wood-type may provide the Fire person with resources; the Fire-type may stimulate the obstinate Earth; Earth may give stability to the rash Metal-type; Metal may give active support to the dreaming Water personality; and Water may provide the knowledge from which the Wood-type is able to create.

Conversely, the Wood-type may will be a drain on the Earth's reserves, perhaps of patience or even materially; an Earth-type could cause damage to Water's reputation; Water may quench the Fire-type's enthusiasm; Fire would be a very formidable opponent for the normally assertive Metal-type, who in turn might harrass Wood.

But what of the future, whatever your animal-type? Chinese astrologers maintain that the success or failure of plans can be foreseen by charting the progress of the Five Elements – whether they are dominant, recessive, waxing or waning: and by comparing the pattern of the Elements of a particular day with those of your own birth-date, Chinese astrologers are able to advise whether the day is likely to prove favourable or otherwise.

Now, with the help of this guide, you will be able to chart your own daily horoscope aspect from the step-by-step instructions given on pages 33–37.

Some people may claim that they do not wish to know what the future holds in store for them. But if there is danger ahead, is it not better to be forewarned? And if there is happiness, will it not give encouragement? Often we are faced with crises and decisions. By perusing your daily horoscope aspect, and taking into consideration the prevailing fortunate elements, problems and dilemmas can often be untangled, and the right direction made clearer.

It is my sincere hope that the knowledge and advice gathered for you from the many friends I have met during my travels to the temples and monasteries throughout China and the Far East will bring you a deeper insight and understanding of your true self, and your relationship with the world about you.

Derek Walters

The *HORSE*

Personality

小牛神將名衞玉卿

*H*orse personalities always feel most comfortable in the company of their own kind, preferring to keep to a circle of established friends, and distrusting strangers. Often, too, they are afraid to mix with, or perhaps more accurately, to be seen mixing with, members of the opposite sex – who are almost regarded as a species apart, either to be worshipped or disdained, but never considered as equals.

[17]

Sporty and sociable, the Horse is the sort of person for whom clubs were invented. Sociability, however, does not rule out competitiveness – although in sports, the Horse usually prefers to participate as a team member rather than as an individual. The Horse likes to be seen as a member of the gang, and not as a loner.

All Horse-types are ready-talkers, though less ready with original ideas. Deep-seated views and prejudices are hard to dislodge. Fond of travel, fashion, and company, Horses thwarted in their ambitions often end up inventing their own life-histories, sometimes attaining a reputation for mild eccentricity.

Born in the Year of the Horse

Neil Armstrong, Billy Graham, Rita Hayworth, Louis Pasteur, Emmeline Pankhurst, Aleksandr Solzhenitsyn

How the Five Elements affect
the *HORSE* Personality

The WOOD-Horse
3 Feb 1954-23 Jan 1955

Under the influence of the Wood element, the Horse personality leans towards rustic, practical, and active pursuits. Such people are much more at home in the countryside, living off the land whenever possible. If they are confined to city living, they become dissatisfied and restless, forever critical of the situation. In love, they belong to the old-fashioned school of romantic chivalry. In marriage, they will make the best of whatever partner comes their way.

The FIRE-Horse
25 Jan 1906-12 Feb 1907,   21 Jan 1966-8 Feb 1967

Fire-Horse children are dreaded throughout Asia, and are traditionally thought of as rebels. They belong to a generation wanting to overthrow the old order. But as parents themselves, they are unlikely to allow their own children the same attitudes. In love, they can be both considerate and demanding. With a Wood partner, life would be volatile; a gentler, if more one-sided existence would occur with a companion born in a Wood year; and the most reliable partnership with an Earth-type.

The EARTH-Horse
11 Feb 1918-31 Jan 1919,   7 Feb 1978-27 Jan 1979

Resolute, and opposed to change, the stubborn Earth-Horse often needs to be goaded into keeping up with the times. The Earth-Horse will not need to strive for promotion as superiors will soon recognize such solid reliability and natural authority. There will be no problem with a partner who is willing to play a subservient role, though with a Fire-type companion there will be greatest happiness.

The METAL-Horse
30 Jan 1930-16 Feb 1931,   27 Jan 1990-14 Feb 1991

The Metal element gives the Horse personality greater business sense. Here is someone who can spot a good business deal, and is able to deal openly with people face-to-face. Romance may take second place to finance. Ideally, therefore, the Metal Horse should choose a partner whose dominant element is either Earth or Water.

The WATER-Horse
15 Feb 1942-4 Feb 1943

The most intellectual of the Horse-types, Water-Horses are fond of conversation, which they often dominate. Such personalities are destined to travel, and likely to adopt a profession which enables them to fulfil this urge. In love, they are restless and unpredictable. If married to a Wood partner, there will be many children.

How the *HORSE*
fares in each animal year

In the Year of the *RAT*, *19 Feb 1996–6 Feb 1997*

This is a most difficult period for the Horse-native, especially if there are to be dealings with people born in the Year of the Rat, who are now at their peak. There could be problems with expenditure. This is definitely not a time for unnecessary risk.

In the Year of the *OX*, *7 Feb 1997–27 Jan 1998*

For the Horse-native, the Year of the Ox is a plodding time; not exactly adverse, but slow and discouraging. Concentrate on family life, and take encouragement from the fact that, next year, matters are going to be greatly improved.

In the Year of the *TIGER*, *28 Jan 1998–15 Feb 1999*

This is a good year for the Horse-personality, involving a great deal of socialising, leading to enhanced business prospects. But it is important to remember that all this social activity is going to cost money: and entertaining, as well as the entertainment, will make heavy demands on resources.

In the Year of the *HARE*, *16 Feb 1999–4 Feb 2000*

The Horse will find this a year of effort. It will be an active time; but in business, while there will be no shortage of work, little financial benefit will follow. In romance, several shallow brief encounters leave a feeling of dissatisfaction. In health, lassitude and depression indicate the need for a respite from the tedium of the moment.

In the Year of the *DRAGON*, *17 Feb 1988–5 Feb 1989*

These born in the Year of the Horse will find this a stimulating year with the promise of foreign travel, and new and exciting projects. In business, the Horse will be offered a challenging position, and this may mean a change of situation. It will be difficult to resist those opportunities which unexpectedly present themselves.

In the Year of the *SNAKE*, *6 Feb 1989–26 Jan 1990*

This is only a moderate year for those born in the Year of the Horse. It is a period of stability rather than expansion, allowing the Horse-type to establish foundations for future dealings. There are no remarkably outstanding business prospects, and romance is marred by jealousy. On the positive side, the time is favourable for home improvements.

In the Year of the *HORSE*, *27 Jan 1990–14 Feb 1991*

This is the Horse's own year, and the world can now be faced with renewed vigour. It is an excellent time for the Horse who wishes to travel; while, at home, any matters connected with the house can be attended to successfully. Luck generally is well-aspected this year.

In the Year of the *SHEEP*, *15 Feb 1991–3 Feb 1992*

The Horse stands to gain this year. In practical terms, it means observing and taking note of what more experienced people have to offer by way of advice. Business prospects look very good, provided that the present course is maintained.

In the Year of the *MONKEY*, *4 Feb 1992–22 Jan 1993*

Since the presence of the Monkey benefits the Horse, a great improvement in conditions may be expected for the Horse-personality this year. Confidence increases, and general health improves. As a result, relationships are strengthened, and renewed enthusiasm at work leads to a broadening of business interests.

In the Year of the *ROOSTER*, *23 Jan 1993–9 Feb 1994*

The Horse-type will go through an irritable phase this year. Much of this derives from the Horse's own conservative personality, for it will be a particularly forward-looking and thrusting time. Matters which do not involve people, however, proceed more favourably.

In the Year of the *DOG*, *10 Feb 1994–30 Jan 1995*

Adventure beckons; and a year of exciting activity lies ahead. For Horse sportsmen and women, this is an ideal record-breaking time. In business, the Horse will pursue deals aggressively, with profitable results. Home and travel both stand prominently in the chart.

In the Year of the *PIG*, *31 Jan 1995–18 Feb 1996*

This will be a moderate year for the Horse-personality, with few gains but little to worry about. New projects can go ahead as planned, bringing positive results in both business and social life. There are problems connected with the house, however, and expenditure on repairs or removals is likely.

HORSE *Relationships*

Find out how you relate to each
of the twelve animal signs, with specific reference
to interaction within the family, in business
and in romance. The tables on pages 46-48
provide a guide to each animal year.

with the Rat Romantically, the chances are that this relationship will blow over, with the partners remaining friends. In business, a clinical, efficient working partnership exists. The Rat-child may appear disappointing in not following the Horse-parent's interests, however.

with the Ox A romantic attachment will come slowly; but, once established, it lasts. In business, too, affairs are rather staid but secure. The Ox-child will prove supportive to the Horse-parent.

with the Tiger This is an exciting choice of partner for the Horse. The Tiger will provide a jet-setting pace, romantically, and in business will help create a very sound and successful career. The Tiger-child will bring the Horse-parent great happiness.

with the Hare The Hare is not the best of partners for the Horse. In business, strife may also occur. A heavy-handed attitude towards the Hare-child will not improve a difficult situation, the Horse will find.

with the Dragon This relationship may provide an exotic life, but beware extravagance. The same stricture applies to business. The Horse-parent may be amused by the Dragon-child's ambitions, but will need to be openly supportive.

with the Snake The Snake and Horse have little in common. The Snake hopes for a more intellectual edge to romantic attachments; while in business, there will be quibbling over details. The Snake-child may disappoint the parental Horse at first, but time will change this and lead to pride.

with another Horse This should be a close-knit partnership, both in romance and in business. The Horse-child will be very loving to the Horse-parent.

with the Sheep In romance, this is a very close attachment and in many ways an ideal partnership, despite many different interests. Horse and Sheep business partners achieve a good working arrangement; and the Sheep-child will be greatly loved by the Horse-parent.

with the Monkey Despite many differences, here is the basis for a long-lasting, if somewhat troubled relationship. Horse and Monkey are more likely to be friends than lovers: but they make an ideal work team. Although the Monkey-child's interests may not follow the Horse-parent's own, they will nevertheless be respected.

with the Rooster This is one of the most successful partnerships. But in a romantic situation, the Rooster may be more concerned with career; and in business, may take over the company. The Rooster-child will be very independent of the Horse-parent.

with the Dog This should be a very happy relationship in terms of romance, and business too. The Dog-child will be very supportive to the parental Horse, meanwhile.

with the Pig The Horse will be content with the Pig's companionship, enjoying domestic bliss. A business relationship should proceed well, too, but may lack inspiration. The Pig-child will provide comfort for the parental Horse.

How the Hour of Birth affects the Fate of the HORSE Personality

Born during the *RAT* hour (11pm-1am)

The Rat hour emphasizes the more negative sides of the Horse's character, leading to strong and immoveable opinions, which often keep friends and others at bay. Personal relationships will have to be worked at particularly hard. In financial matters, however, there is ample success.

Born during the *OX* hour (1am-3am)

In any matters concerning the use of land – as distinct from dealing in real estate – rewards are secure. Wealth is to be found in the country rather than in the city. Avoid speculation, although legal matters will succeed. Romance is not your first consideration.

Born during the *TIGER* hour (3am-5am)

Success will come from any concerns which involve journeys and distribution. Other trades and professions are poorly aspected. Children may be seldom seen, but a good marriage is likely.

Born during the *HARE* hour (5am-7am)

Health matters have an important role to play throughout life; and it is possible that a career connected with medicine or nursing will be considered. In romance, there may be unhappiness, but children will bring great contentment.

Born during the *DRAGON* hour (7am-9am)

Several strokes of good fortune may tempt you into gambling. If money is your first consideration, career, romance and family will take a low place in the list of priorities. Apply yourself diligently at work and you will find great personal happiness.

Born during the *SNAKE* hour (9am-11am)

You are likely to follow a practical career which demands the application of intelligence. Paper-work, however, will not be a strong point, as preference is for an outdoor life. Romance, family, and children may bring some problems. Health is sound.

Born during the *HORSE* hour (11am-1pm)

Sociability and sportiveness are emphasized, as is a tendency to being shy of the opposite sex. In romance, you may have many shallow dalliances; but having found true love, you will remain faithful for life. Success tends to come second-hand. In business and career, stick to well-established concerns.

Born during the *SHEEP* hour (1pm-3pm)

Romantic aspirations combine with sound practicality to produce a marriage built on good, solid foundations. Domestic harmony leads to success in business, and capable children. Avoid speculation.

Born during the *MONKEY* hour (3pm-5pm)

If you have personal skills and special abilities, use them, as they will bring wealth. Your love-life will be rich and varied, which may result in an unwillingness to settle down. Avoid activities which may not appear strictly legal, as the aspects in this direction are poor.

Born during the *ROOSTER* hour (5pm-7pm)

Although a career in the performing arts is considered, many difficulties stand in the way, particularly as there is such competition. Take care not to offend possible supporters whose help you may need later. In romance, be prepared for disillusion. Success is shown in business and commerce.

Born during the *DOG* hour (7pm-9pm)

The position regarding property and inheritance is very favourable. Disappointment in love may be followed by life in a foreign country, and this may lead to marriage there. Take special care with any speculative activities.

Born during the *PIG* hour (9pm-11pm)

A solid, domestic background is indicated, with an old-fashioned, well-ordered family. Finances are secure, and health is sound.

Casting a daily horoscope

*T*he Chinese have always been very down-to-earth in their approach to astrology; and while they find it fascinating to learn about their inner selves and to know how they stand in their personal relationships, they are much more likely to expect an astrologer to give them sound, practical advice on everyday matters.

Chinese astrology is certainly able to do much more than reveal the complexities of your personality. Indeed, by drafting an individual daily horoscope forecast, it is possible to discover which days will be best suited for business and social life, when you may need to take special care, when you would do best to stay at home rather than embarking on a long journey, or when you are likely to meet with particularly good fortune.

On the pages that follow, you will find the basic method for casting your own personal daily horoscope, carefully set out, step by step. No mathematical prowess is needed, just an ability to add and subtract a few simple figures. These straightforward calculations will enable you to find the cyclic number for your date of birth, and any other date this century. (These numbers are an exact match with those published in the official Chinese astrological calendar, the oldest in the world, and still in continuous use after more than three thousand years.) These two numbers are then compared to find the *aspect number* which reveals the daily forecast given in the final section.

How to Calculate Your Own Personal Daily Horoscope Aspect

(Note: The Chinese day begins at 11pm: so if you were born between 11pm and midnight, base your calculations on the day following your birthdate.)

Take a piece of paper, preferably lined, and write the letters A to K in a column down the left-hand side.

Finding the cyclic number for your date of birth

[A] At A on your sheet of paper, write the *date* of the month of your birth: i.e. if you were born on 12th April, write 12.

[B] Using Table I on page 45, find the code number for your month of birth and write this at B.

[C] Using Table II on page 45, find the code number for your year of birth and write this at C.

[D] If you were born on or after February 29th during a leap-year, put 1 at D. Otherwise put O. (A leap year is one which is divisible by 4; 1988 is therefore a leap year).

[E] Add the figures at A, B, C and D.
If the result is 121 or more, subtract 120; if the figure is between 61 and 120, subtract 60. Write the result at E.

This is the *cyclic number for your birthdate*.

Finding the cyclic number for any date this century

You will need to follow the same procedure outlined in steps A to D to find the cyclic number for any required day this century.

[F] Write the *date* of the month of the required date at F.

[G] Write the *monthly* code number for the required month at G.

[H] Write the *yearly* code number for the required year at H.

[I] Write the figure 1 at I, if a leap-year adjustment is required. Otherwise put O.

[J] Add the figures at F, G, H and I.

If the total is 121 or more, subtract 120; if the figure is between 61 and 120, subtract 60. Write the result at J.

This is the *cyclic number for the required date*.

Finding your personal daily aspect number

First note whether the cyclic number for your birthdate (E) is *yang* (an *odd* number) or *yin* (an even number.)

(i) If the cyclic number for your birthdate (E) is *yang* (odd):
      from the cyclic number for the required date (J)
      SUBTRACT
      the cyclic number for the birthdate (E).
      (Note. If J is less then E, first add 60.)
      Write your result at K.

(ii) If the cyclic number for your birthdate (E) is *yin* (even):
      from the cyclic number for the birthdate (E)
      SUBTRACT
      the cyclic number for the required date (J).
      (Note. If E is less than J, first add 60.)
      Write your result at K.

The figure at K is your *Personal Daily Aspect Number*. Now turn to pages 38–44 to find your own personal forecast for the required date.

Your Personal Daily Horoscope Aspects

[0] *See aspect 60.*

[1] There are highly favourable prospects for the Horse today, and it is an excellent time for leisure activities, socialising, visiting friends, or attending functions.

[2] The Horse will find this to be an excellent day for commercial transactions generally, and there are particularly encouraging results in any matters involving younger members of the family.

[3] Although this is generally a favourable day for all kinds of activity, there may be some set-backs with regards to commercial transactions. It is a good day for forward planning.

[4] Try to take things easily today. Hasty decisions lead to regrets. There is a fortunate response to business correspondence.

[5] This is an ideal day for practical activities, and extremely favourable for home changes and anything involving construction, interior work, or mechanical matters.

[6] This is a good, steady day when you will have confidence in both business and personal relationships. There are also highly favourable prospects for your family concerns.

[7] Avoid making plans for your personal life today. You will be best working away from the home, but do not waste time in any unnecessary travelling.

[8] There could be set-backs today in dealings with colleagues,

family, or circumstances where you have to assert yourself. There will be success with respect to changes at home.

[9] It will be a smooth running day, but take advice regarding legal and business matters.

[10] Matters today remain fairly stable. This enables you to proceed on your chosen course without interruption.

[11] Conditions remain generally unchanged. Dismiss minor irritations for what they are. Persevere, and you will get the results you wanted.

[12] It is an ideal day for matters relating to friends, while romance is also a possibility. Renewed strength and confidence will help you to obtain your objectives.

[13] You may find yourself involved in a lot of strenuous leisure activity today, as the accent appears to be on enjoyment. It is a favourable time for the signing of documents.

[14] This is a good day for interviews, especially if you are thinking of visiting someone for advice on your health or general well-being.

[15] Plans regarding the home and matters relating to friends go well today. Take care over finances, however.

[16] Try not to get involved in open-ended situations. Plan ahead carefully, and keep objectives short-term. The morning is better for any commercial transactions.

[17] Conditions are very favourable today for home and family matters. Personal correspondence, reading, and study will prove rewarding for you.

[18] You will meet with success in both business and personal matters today. But rethink your leisure plans.

[19] An apparently straightforward matter may involve a great deal of activity today, but the results will be successful. Be prepared for certain changes.

[20] Proceed with confidence in respect of your business interests. Avoid gambling, or anything involving financial risk, however.

[21] Use the present stable conditions to their best advantage. This is a good time for looking over any contracts involving the home, or family legal matters.

[22] The Horse will find this an ideal day for short journeys. But conditions are less ideal for routine matters.

[23] You will have some exciting ideas regarding improvements at home which you should follow up. Business runs well; but today is much better for routine work.

[24] You may need to take advice regarding someone in your family, but leave any decision for a while. Try not to be persuaded against your better judgement, and weigh up the helpful suggestions which you have received.

[25] This is an ideal day for most matters, especially if travelling is involved; but in legal matters the position is less secure. There is a chance of promotion.

[26] Do not act too hastily regarding relationships. Your leisure plans will be quite enjoyable.

[27] The Horse's prospects for today continue to improve, though there may be a few obstacles regarding commercial transactions. There is the prospect of a better financial position for those able to make time available for study.

[28] While the day passes peacably enough, you will not get through everything you wanted to do. However, you can still proceed with a degree of confidence.

[29] There could be obstacles ahead, so be prepared to put a lot of effort into your activities today. Take advice on any matters concerning children. A chance meeting could well lead to friendship.

[30] You may feel like making changes to your plans. Act on any ideas you have, and use your contacts.

[31] There will be moderate success with respect to the household. Keep on sure ground, and stick to family matters. This is a particularly demanding day.

[32] It will be a good day for you to try to improve your image. Now that finances are more secure, there is the chance to buy something you always wanted.

[33] Conditions are favourable for all matters to do with the home and personal life. Use your knowledge of present conditions to put your plans into action.

[34] There is an improved position with respect to career prospects, but generally little change. It is a good day for selling, and also for anything concerning personal appearance.

[35] This is a very mixed day, when exciting promises are off-set by disappointments. Avoid dealing with legal matters.

[36] Take care when dealing with casual acquaintances. Do not involve them in your personal problems. Business and commercial activities fare successfully today.

[37] For most activities, it will be a particularly demanding, but nevertheless highly successful day. There may be problems in your personal life, however.

[38] There are highly favourable prospects for matters concerning land, and all long-term projects which have been established for some time. Plan any journeys carefully.

[39] It would be advisable not to get too involved today in situations where the people are not known to you personally. Take advice if you are worried about your health.

[40] For the Horse, this will be an average day. No areas are particularly highlighted, but neither are there any dangerous pitfalls. The early evening will bring interesting news.

[41] While all signs are for the most part favourable, there will be greater expenditure than expected today. You will, however, achieve your objectives.

[42] It is important to take care today not to strain your resources – physical and financial. Keep away from personal confrontation, and avoid unnecessary travel.

[43] This is an excellent day for achieving person ambitions. All practical matters will be successful.

[44] Although this is not an outstanding day in your diary, there is a pleasant surprise in store for you.

[45] The Horse is unlikely to get through today without argument and some wrangling, and will have to work hard to succeed.

[46] Although today's achievements will be below par, you will find you have a renewed vitality and gain greater inner confidence.

[47] Today will be an exhausting one, but it also brings great benefits. Expect greater demands on you at work, leading to possible promotion. Dealings with employees or subordinates will also progress very well.

[48] Conditions are not favourable at the moment for getting things done, even though you may feel in a creative mood. It is a better day for planning than achieving. Do not take financial risks today.

[49] Matters remain fairly stable, with little difference in conditions generally at home or at work. This enables you to get on with the task in hand without distractions.

[50] The Horse will find this a good day for team activities; but social events are best when they are with colleagues rather than family. Expect some setbacks, and put down losses to experience.

[51] This will be an enjoyable day, but be prepared for an unexpected call on your finances. You are likely to be asked to join in some socializing to celebrate a friend's success.

[52] Matters may go smoothly at work, but there may be upsets at home. Be prepared for a frustrating time, and keep your head.

[53] It will be a favourable day for personal achievement. Some

unexpected financial reward is also foreseen.

[54] It is a good day for romance and leisure. In solid, practical matters, however, conditions are unfavourable. Avoid becoming anxious over temporary setbacks, and try not to take matters too seriously.

[55] Anything to do with the house or family is highlighted for the Horse today. It is also an excellent time for buying or selling land, or for signing contracts to do with the home or its furnishings. There will be good news too, regarding health matters, either for yourself or your family.

[56] This is an above average day, which sees you feeling physical improvement. There will be ideal conditions at home.

[57] It is not one of your best days. Be careful in your dealings with others, whether on a romantic, social or business level. Try and avoid situations which are going to demand your best responses, too.

[58] Although practically you may not achieve much today, you will have laid the groundwork for future expansion. On the face of it, there will be little to show, but you will be inwardly satisfied by the day's progress.

[59] Conditions are generally unchanged, which will enable you to go ahead as planned.

[60][0] Proceed with confidence to achieve your ambitions. Prospects for health, travel, home-life, business and romance are all excellent.

TABLE I
Code number for the month

Month	Jan	Feb	Mar	April	May	June	July	Aug	Sept	Oct	Nov	Dec
Code	0	31	59	30	0	31	1	32	3	35	4	34

TABLE II
Code number for the year

Year	1901	1902	1903	1904	1905	1906	1907	1908	1909	1910	1911	1912
Code	15	20	25	30	36	41	46	51	57	2	7	12

Year	1913	1914	1915	1916	1917	1918	1919	1920	1921	1922	1923	1924
Code	18	23	28	33	39	44	49	54	0	5	10	15

Year	1925	1926	1927	1928	1929	1930	1931	1932	1933	1934	1935	1936
Code	21	26	31	36	42	47	52	57	3	8	13	18

Year	1937	1938	1939	1940	1941	1942	1943	1944	1945	1946	1947	1948
Code	24	29	34	39	45	50	55	0	6	11	16	21

Year	1949	1950	1951	1952	1953	1954	1955	1956	1957	1958	1959	1960
Code	27	32	37	42	48	53	58	3	9	14	19	24

Year	1961	1962	1963	1964	1965	1966	1967	1968	1969	1970	1971	1972
Code	30	35	40	45	51	56	1	6	12	17	22	27

Year	1973	1974	1975	1976	1977	1978	1979	1980	1981	1982	1983	1984
Code	33	38	43	48	54	59	4	9	15	20	25	30

Year	1985	1986	1987	1988	1989	1990	1991	1992	1993	1994	1995	1996
Code	36	41	46	51	57	2	7	12	18	23	28	33

Year	1997	1998	1999	2000
Code	39	44	49	54

The Chinese Calendar

19 Feb 1901 – 7 Feb 1902
Metal-Ox

10 Feb 1910 – 29 Jan 1911
Metal-Dog

1 Feb 1919 – 19 Feb 1920
Earth-Sheep

8 Feb 1902 – 28 Jan 1903
Water-Tiger

30 Jan 1911 – 17 Feb 1912
Metal-Pig

20 Feb 1920 – 7 Feb 1921
Metal-Monkey

29 Jan 1903 – 15 Feb 1904
Water-Hare

18 Feb 1912 – 5 Feb 1913
Water-Rat

8 Feb 1921 – 27 Jan 1922
Metal-Rooster

16 Feb 1904 – 3 Feb 1905
Wood-Dragon

6 Feb 1913 – 25 Jan 1914
Water-Ox

28 Jan 1922 – 15 Feb 1923
Water-Dog

4 Feb 1905 – 24 Jan 1906
Wood-Snake

26 Jan 1914 – 13 Feb 1915
Wood-Tiger

16 Feb 1923 – 4 Feb 1924
Water-Pig

25 Jan 1906 – 12 Feb 1907
Fire-Horse

14 Feb 1915 – 2 Feb 1916
Wood-Hare

5 Feb 1924 – 24 Jan 1925
Wood-Rat

13 Feb 1907 – 1 Feb 1908
Fire-Sheep

3 Feb 1916 – 22 Jan 1917
Fire-Dragon

25 Jan 1925 – 12 Feb 1926
Wood-Ox

2 Feb 1908 – 21 Jan 1909
Earth-Monkey

23 Jan 1917 – 10 Feb 1918
Fire-Snake

13 Feb 1926 – 1 Feb 1927
Fire-Tiger

22 Jan 1909 – 9 Feb 1910
Earth-Rooster

11 Feb 1918 – 31 Jan 1919
Earth-Horse

2 Feb 1927 – 22 Jan 1928
Fire-Hare

23 Jan 1928 – 9 Feb 1929
Earth-Dragon

10 Feb 1929 – 29 Jan 1930
Earth-Snake

30 Jan 1930 – 16 Feb 1931
Metal-Horse

17 Feb 1931 – 5 Feb 1932
Metal-Sheep

6 Feb 1932 – 25 Jan 1933
Water-Monkey

26 Jan 1933 – 13 Feb 1934
Water-Rooster

14 Feb 1934 – 3 Feb 1935
Wood-Dog

4 Feb 1935 – 23 Jan 1936
Wood-Pig

24 Jan 1936 – 10 Feb 1937
Fire-Rat

11 Feb 1937 – 30 Jan 1938
Fire-Ox

31 Jan 1938 – 18 Feb 1939
Earth-Tiger

19 Feb 1939 – 7 Feb 1940
Earth-Hare

8 Feb 1940 – 26 Jan 1941
Metal-Dragon

27 Jan 1941 – 14 Feb 1942
Metal-Snake

15 Feb 1942 – 4 Feb 1943
Water-Horse

5 Feb 1943 – 24 Jan 1944
Water-Sheep

25 Jan 1944 – 12 Feb 1945
Wood-Monkey

13 Feb 1945 – 1 Feb 1946
Wood-Rooster

2 Feb 1946 – 21 Jan 1947
Fire-Dog

22 Jan 1947 – 9 Feb 1948
Fire-Pig

10 Feb 1948 – 28 Jan 1949
Earth-Rat

29 Jan 1949 – 16 Feb 1950
Earth-Ox

17 Feb 1950 – 5 Feb 1951
Metal-Tiger

6 Feb 1951 – 26 Jan 1952
Metal-Hare

27 Jan 1952 – 13 Feb 1953
Water-Dragon

14 Feb 1953 – 2 Feb 1954
Water-Snake

3 Feb 1954 – 23 Jan 1955
Wood-Horse

24 Jan 1955 – 11 Feb 1956
Wood-Sheep

12 Feb 1956 – 30 Jan 1957
Fire-Monkey

31 Jan 1957 – 17 Feb 1958
Fire-Rooster

18 Feb 1958 – 7 Feb 1959
Earth-Dog

8 Feb 1959 – 27 Jan 1960
Earth-Pig

28 Jan 1960 – 14 Feb 1961
Metal-Rat

15 Feb 1961 – 4 Feb 1962
Metal-Ox

5 Feb 1962 – 24 Jan 1963
Water-Tiger

25 Jan 1963 – 12 Feb 1964
Water-Hare

13 Feb 1964 – 1 Feb 1965
Wood-Dragon

2 Feb 1965 – 20 Jan 1966
Wood-Snake

21 Jan 1966 – 8 Feb 1967
Fire-Horse

9 Feb 1967 – 29 Jan 1968
Fire-Sheep

30 Jan 1968 – 16 Feb 1969
Earth-Monkey

17 Feb 1969 – 5 Feb 1970
Earth-Rooster

6 Feb 1970 – 26 Jan 1971
Metal-Dog

27 Jan 1971 – 14 Feb 1972
Metal-Pig

15 Feb 1972 – 2 Feb 1973
Water-Rat

3 Feb 1973 – 22 Jan 1974
Water-Ox

23 Jan 1974 – 10 Feb 1975
Wood-Tiger

11 Feb 1975 – 30 Jan 1976
Wood-Hare

31 Jan 1976 – 17 Feb 1977
Fire-Dragon

18 Feb 1977 – 6 Feb 1978
Fire-Snake

7 Feb 1978 – 27 Jan 1979
Earth-Horse

28 Jan 1979 – 15 Feb 1980
Earth-Sheep

16 Feb 1980 – 4 Feb 1981
Metal-Monkey

5 Feb 1981 – 24 Jan 1982
Metal-Rooster

25 Jan 1982 – 12 Feb 1983
Water-Dog

13 Feb 1983 – 1 Feb 1984
Water-Pig

2 Feb 1984 – 19 Feb 1985
Wood-Rat

20 Feb 1985 – 8 Feb 1986
Wood-Ox

9 Feb 1986 – 28 Jan 1987
Fire-Tiger

29 Jan 1987 – 16 Feb 1988
Fire-Hare

17 Feb 1988 – 5 Feb 1989
Earth-Dragon

6 Feb 1989 – 26 Jan 1990
Earth-Snake

27 Jan 1990 – 14 Feb 1991
Metal-Horse

15 Feb 1991 – 3 Feb 1992
Metal-Sheep

4 Feb 1992 – 22 Jan 1993
Water-Monkey

23 Jan 1993 – 9 Feb 1994
Water-Rooster

10 Feb 1994 – 30 Jan 1995
Wood-Dog

31 Jan 1995 – 18 Feb 1996
Wood-Pig

19 Feb 1996 – 6 Feb 1997
Fire-Rat

7 Feb 1997 – 27 Jan 1998
Fire-Ox

28 Jan 1998 – 15 Feb 1999
Earth-Tiger

16 Feb 1999 – 4 Feb 2000
Earth-Hare